WRITING THE
BILL OF RIGHTS

BY MATT BOWERS

AMICUS | AMICUS INK

Sequence is published by Amicus and Amicus Ink
P.O. Box 1329, Mankato, MN 56002
www.amicuspublishing.us

Library of Congress Cataloging-in-Publication Data
Names: Bowers, Matt, author.
Title: Writing the Bill of Rights / by Matt Bowers.
Description: Mankato, Minnesota : Amicus, [2020] | Series: Sequence American Government | Includes index.
Identifiers: LCCN 2018039486 (print) | LCCN 2018040105 (ebook) | ISBN 9781681517537 (pdf) | ISBN 9781681516714 (library binding) | ISBN 9781681524573 (pbk.)
Subjects: LCSH: United States. Constitution. 1st-10th Amendments--Juvenile literature. | Civil rights--United States--Juvenile literature.
Classification: LCC KF4749 (ebook) | LCC KF4749 .B69 2020 (print) | DDC 342.7303/9--dc23
LC record available at https://lccn.loc.gov/2018039486

Editor: Alissa Thielges
Designer: Veronica Scott
Photo Researcher: Holly Young

Photo Credits: Getty/Bettmann cover, 22; iStock/leezsnow cover; Getty/Pacific Press 5; Alamy/Pictures Now 6; Public Domain Pictures/Lydia Jacobs 6–7; Getty/Stock Montage 9; WikiCommons/Howard Chandler Christy 10–11; Alamy/North Wind Picture Archives 12–13; WikiCommons/Ferdinand Richardt 14–15; Getty/Stock Montage 17; Library of Congress/National Archives Catalog 18; Flickr/USCapitol/Architect of the Capitol 21; Shutterstock/Bill Chizek 25; iStock/StephanieCraig 26–27; AP/Dana Verkouteren 29

Printed in the United States of America

HC 10 9 8 7 6 5 4 3 2 1
PB 10 9 8 7 6 5 4 3 2 1

TABLE OF CONTENTS

The Bill of Rights

People in the United States have a lot of freedoms. We can express our opinions. If we don't like the president, we can say so. We can hold peaceful protests. We can worship how we want to. These are our **rights**. Our nation adopted them over 200 years ago. They are part of the U.S. Constitution. They are called the Bill of Rights.

LOADING...LOADING...LOADIN

People protest a new law. The Bill of Rights protects this right.

LOADING.. LOADING.. LOADING...

Each state had its own set of laws. This shaped how each citizen lived.

Articles of Confederation create a weak national government.

MARCH 1, 1781

LOADING...LOADING...

A New Nation

In early U.S. history, there was no central government. The states were not united. To unite the states, a national government was needed. The Articles of Confederation were created. This loosely bound the states together. By March 1, 1781, every state had approved it. A central government was in place. But it was weak. It couldn't govern very well.

LOADING...LOADING...LOADING...

In 1787, a group of 55 people from the states came together. They are called the **framers**. They wrote the U.S. Constitution. This created a strong **federal** government. But there was no bill of rights. This is a list of rights that belong to the people. Most states had one. Some framers wanted one in the U.S. Constitution, too.

Articles of Confederation create a weak national government.

MARCH 1, 1781   1787

NG . . . LOADING . . .

Framers write the
U.S. Constitution.

The framers are also called founding fathers.

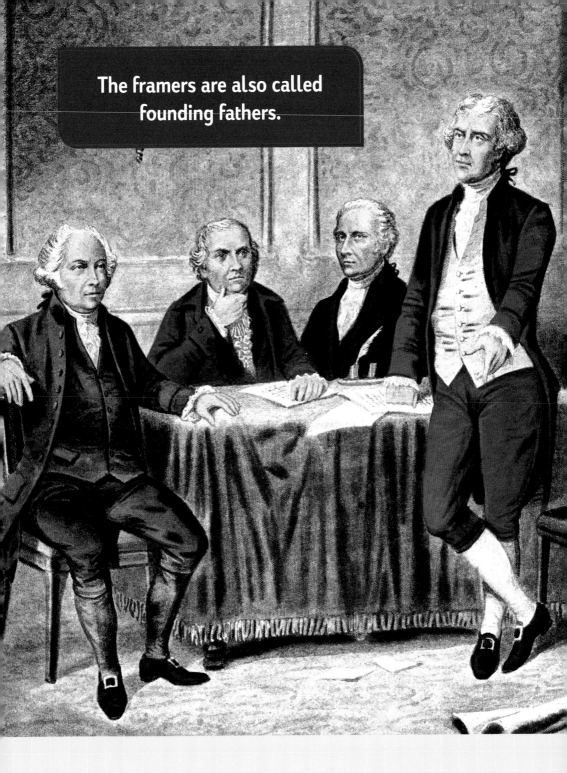

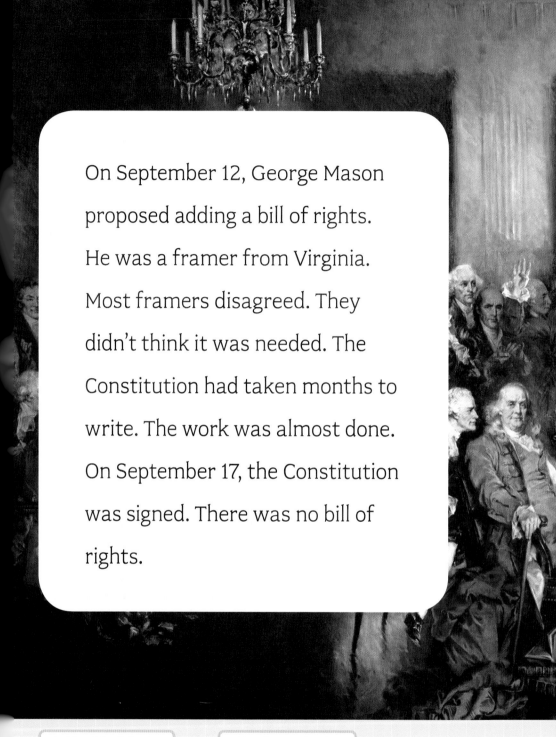

On September 12, George Mason proposed adding a bill of rights. He was a framer from Virginia. Most framers disagreed. They didn't think it was needed. The Constitution had taken months to write. The work was almost done. On September 17, the Constitution was signed. There was no bill of rights.

Articles of Confederation create a weak national government.

Most framers sign the Constitution, which didn't have a bill of rights.

MARCH 1, 1781   1787   SEPT. 17, 1787   LOADING...

Framers write the U.S. Constitution.

Thirty-nine framers signed the Constitution. Some framers were absent or chose not to sign.

The framers debated adding a bill of rights to the Constitution. Would it become law?

Framers write the Constitution.

Articles of Confederation create a weak national government.

Most framers sign the Constitution, which didn't have a bill of rights.

The states argue whether a bill of rights is needed.

MARCH 1, 1781   1787   SEPT. 17, 1787   1787

Framers write the U.S. Constitution.

For the Constitution to become law, 9 of 13 states had to **ratify** it. The states held big meetings. Leaders debated. The **federalists** supported it. They thought the Constitution was good enough. It would protect the rights of the people.

Others did not agree. They worried the federal government would take away people's rights. They wanted a bill of rights.

To move forward, the federalists made a promise. A bill of rights would be added after the new government was set up. Did this work? Yes! By June 21, 1788, nine states had ratified the Constitution. There was a new federal government! Next, Congress got started on a bill of rights.

Articles of Confederation create a weak national government.

Most framers sign the Constitution, which didn't have a bill of rights.

Ninth state ratifies Constitution; new federal government is created.

MARCH 1, 1781   1787   SEPT. 17, 1787   1787   JUNE 21, 1788

Framers write the U.S. Constitution.

The states argue whether a bill of rights is needed.

Congress first met in New York, then moved to Congress Hall (above) in Philadelphia.

Creating the Bill of Rights

In 1789, the **House of Representatives** worked on the Bill of Rights. Another framer from Virginia led the effort. His name was James Madison. He knew this was important to the people. He had a list of ideas from the states. On June 8, 1789, he proposed the ideas as **amendments** to the Constitution. They included freedom of religion, speech, and the press, along with many other rights.

Articles of Confederation create a weak national government.

Most framers sign the Constitution, which didn't have a bill of rights.

Ninth state ratifies Constitution; new fed government is creat

MARCH 1, 1781   **1787**   **SEPT. 17, 1787**   **1787**   **JUNE 21, 1788**

Framers write the U.S. Constitution.

The states argue whether a bill of rights is needed.

Madison was a federalist. But he knew a bill of rights would help people support the new government.

JUNE 8, 1789

LOADING...LOADING...

James Madison proposes amendments in the House.

CONGRESS OF THE UNITED STATES.

In the HOUSE *of* REPRESENTATIVES,

Monday, 24th August, 1789.

concurring

RESOLVED, BY THE SENATE AND HOUSE OF REPRESENTA-
TIVES OF THE UNITED STATES OF AMERICA IN CONGRESS
ASSEMBLED, two thirds of both Houses deeming it necessary, That
the following Articles be proposed to the Legislatures of the several
States, as Amendments to the Constitution of the United States, all
or any of which Articles, when ratified by three fourths of the said
Legislatures, to be valid to all intents and purposes as part of the
said Constitution—Viz.

ARTICLES in addition to, and amendment of, the Constitution of
the United States of America, proposed by Congress, and ratified
by the Legislatures of the several States, pursuant to the fifth Article of the original Constitution.

ARTICLE THE FIRST.

After the first enumeration, required by the first Article of the
Constitution, there shall be one Representative for every thirty thousand, until the number shall amount to one hundred, after which
the proportion shall be so regulated by Congress, that there shall
be not less than one hundred Representatives, nor less than one Representative for every forty thousand persons, until the number of
Representatives shall amount to two hundred, after which the proportion shall be so regulated by Congress, that there shall not be less
than two hundred Representatives, nor less than one Representative
for every fifty thousand persons.

amendment

ARTICLE THE SECOND.

No law varying the compensation to the members of Congress,
shall take effect, until an election of Representatives shall have in-
tervened.

a

ARTICLE THE THIRD.

Congress shall make no law establishing religion or prohibiting
the free exercise thereof, nor shall the rights of Conscience be infringed.

Articles of Faith or a mode of Worship, or prohibiting the free exercise of Religion.

Congress shall make no law abridging

ARTICLE THE FOURTH.

The Freedom of Speech, and of the Press, and the right of the
People peaceably to assemble,
and to apply to the Government for a redress of grievances, shall
not be infringed.

petition

Articles of Confederation create a weak national government.

Most framers sign the Constitution, which didn't have a bill of rights.

Ninth state ratifies Constitution; new federal government is created.

MARCH 1, 1781   1787   SEPT. 17, 1787   1787   JUNE 21, 1788

Framers write the U.S. Constitution.

The states argue whether a bill of rights is needed.

The amendments needed some work. For this, the House made the Committee of Eleven. Each state had one member, except Rhode Island and North Carolina. Those states had yet to ratify the Constitution. The Committee of Eleven worked in July. They made some changes. Their final report was sent back to the House.

Changes were written on the bill before being sent back to Congress.

The Committee of Eleven works on the proposed amendments.

JUNE 8, 1789   JULY 1789   ING . . . LOADING . . .

James Madison proposes amendments in the House.

It is not easy to change the Constitution. An amendment needs a two-thirds vote in both the House and the Senate to pass. This took awhile. There was a lot of debate. The House made changes. So did the Senate. Then they both worked on the changes together. At last, by September 25, 1789, 12 amendments had passed.

Articles of Confederation create a weak national government.

Most framers sign the Constitution, which didn't have a bill of rights.

Ninth state ratifies Constitution; new federal government is created.

MARCH 1, 1781   1787   SEPT. 17, 1787   1787   JUNE 21, 1788

Framers write the U.S. Constitution.

The states argue whether a bill of rights is needed.

The First Congress passed 12 amendments to the Constitution.

The Committee of Eleven works on the proposed amendments.

JUNE 8, 1789   JULY 1789   SEPT. 25, 1789

LOADING...

James Madison proposes amendments in the House.

Congress passes 12 amendments to the U.S. Constitution.

21

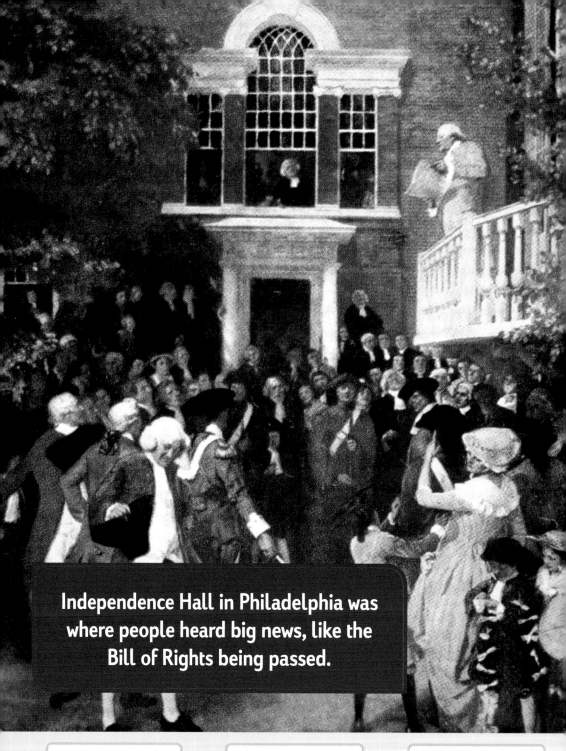

Independence Hall in Philadelphia was where people heard big news, like the Bill of Rights being passed.

Articles of Confederation create a weak national government.

Most framers sign the Constitution, which didn't have a bill of rights.

Ninth state ratifies Constitution; new federal government is created.

MARCH 1, 1781   1787   SEPT. 17, 1787   1787   JUNE 21, 1788

Framers write the U.S. Constitution.

The states argue whether a bill of rights is needed.

Next, it was the states' turn. Three-fourths of the states needed to ratify them. This is how amendments become law. By December 15, 1791, 10 amendments were ratified. They became law! The other two were not. These first 10 became the Bill of Rights. They were added to the Constitution.

The Committee of Eleven works on the proposed amendments.

Ten amendments are ratified by states; called the Bill of Rights.

JUNE 8, 1789   JULY 1789   SEPT. 25, 1789   DEC. 15, 1791

James Madison proposes amendments in the House.

Congress passes 12 amendments to the U.S. Constitution.

Our Rights Today

Over the years people have disagreed. What does the Bill of Rights mean? We can't ask the framers. So who decides? The federal courts do. They have the final say. Judges study the laws and know each amendment. They **interpret** the Constitution. They decide how it applies in certain cases. Their **rulings** shape the Bill of Rights.

Articles of Confederation create a weak national government.

Most framers sign the Constitution, which didn't have a bill of rights.

Ninth state ratifies Constitution; new federal government is created.

MARCH 1, 1781   1787   SEPT. 17, 1787   1787   JUNE 21, 1788

Framers write the U.S. Constitution.

The states argue whether a bill of rights is needed.

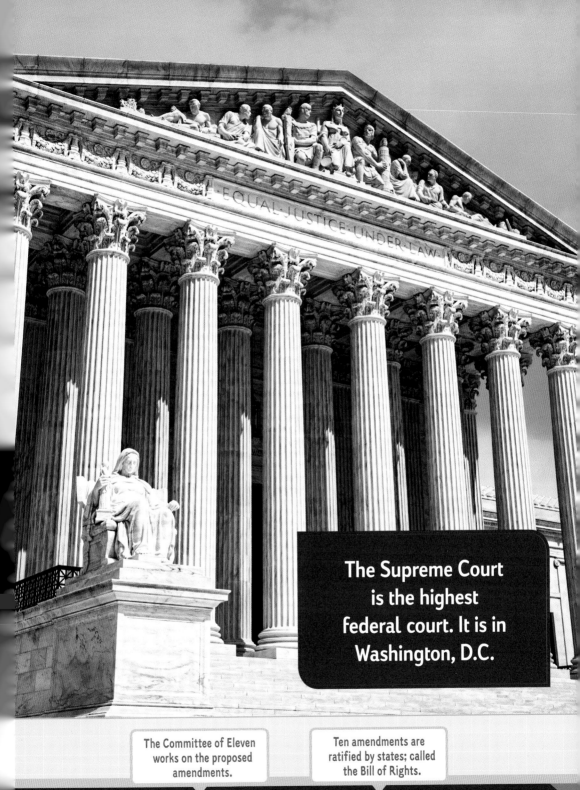

The Supreme Court is the highest federal court. It is in Washington, D.C.

The Committee of Eleven works on the proposed amendments.

Ten amendments are ratified by states; called the Bill of Rights.

JUNE 8, 1789   JULY 1789   SEPT. 25, 1789   DEC. 15, 1791

James Madison proposes amendments in the House.

Congress passes 12 amendments to the U.S. Constitution.

CONGRESS SHALL MAKE NO LAW *respecting an establishment of religion, or prohibiting the free exercise thereof; or abridging the freedom of speech, or of the press; or the right of the people peaceably to assemble, and to petition the Government for a redress of grievances.*

❦ THE FIRST AMENDMENT TO THE U.S. CONSTITUTION
15 DECEMBER 1791

Articles of Confederation create a weak national government.

Most framers sign the Constitution, which didn't have a bill of rights.

Ninth state ratifies Constitution; new federal government is created.

MARCH 1, 1781   **1787**   **SEPT. 17, 1787**   **1787**   **JUNE 21, 1788**

Framers write the U.S. Constitution.

The states argue whether a bill of rights is needed.

The Bill of Rights is old, but it is a powerful document. It hasn't changed in more than 225 years. We still exercise the rights listed in it every day. When a newspaper publishes a story, that is freedom of the press. When you share your opinion, you are exercising free speech. It is important to know your rights. They are freedoms that belong to every person in America.

The First Amendment text is carved in stone outside of Independence Hall.

The Committee of Eleven works on the proposed amendments.

Ten amendments are ratified by states; called the Bill of Rights.

JUNE 8, 1789   JULY 1789   SEPT. 25, 1789   DEC. 15, 1791   TODAY

James Madison proposes amendments in the House.

Congress passes 12 amendments to the U.S. Constitution.

American people exercise their rights.

27

What's in the Bill of Rights?

First Amendment

No law shall prevent the freedoms of religion, speech, and press, or the right for people to petition and assemble peacefully.

Second Amendment

People have a right to keep and bear weapons to maintain a free state and orderly **militia**.

Third Amendment

In times of peace, people don't have to house soldiers if they don't want to.

Fourth Amendment

Police need a **warrant** to look at or take away anything you own. A warrant will only be granted if there is a reason.

Fifth Amendment

A person's rights will not be taken away without a fair trial. You do not have to testify against yourself.

Sixth Amendment

An accused person has the right to know what they did wrong. Criminal cases will have a fast and public trial by a jury of peers.

Seventh Amendment

In a federal civil case, people can have a jury trial.

Eighth Amendment

Bails and court fines can't be extreme. Cruel and unusual punishment is not allowed.

Ninth Amendment

The Bill of Rights is not a complete list. The people may have other rights that are not listed.

Tenth Amendment

Powers not listed in the Constitution belong to the states and people.

The U.S. Supreme Court hears a case. They interpret the Bill of Rights.

Glossary

amendment A change or addition to the U.S. Constitution.

federal Relating to a type of government where states are united under one central power but also have their own governments and can make their own laws.

federalist A person in favor of a strong federal government.

framer A person who helped write the U.S. Constitution.

House of Representatives One of two houses in the U.S. Congress that makes laws; the number of members from each state is based on population.

interpret To decide and explain what something means; U.S. courts interpret the Constitution.

militia A group of local people trained to act as a military force in times of emergency.

ratify To officially approve.

right Something a person is legally entitled to do.

ruling The official decision or judgment made by a judge in a court case.

Senate One of two houses in the U.S. Congress that makes laws; each state has two U.S. senators.

warrant An official piece of paper that gives police permission to do something.

Read More

Harris, Nancy. *What's the Bill of Rights?* Chicago: Heinemann, 2016.

Krull, Kathleen. *A Kid's Guide to America's Bill of Rights.* New York: HarperCollins, 2015.

Leavitt, Amie Jane. *The Bill of Rights in Translation: What It Really Means.* North Mankato, Minn.: Capstone Press, 2018.

Lynch, Seth. *The Bill of Rights.* New York: Gareth Stevens Publishing, 2019.

Websites

Bill of Rights of the United States of America (1791)
http://billofrightsinstitute.org/founding-documents/bill-of-rights/

Learning Adventures—Bill of Rights: 1789-91
https://bensguide.gpo.gov/bill-of-rights-1789-91

Writing Rights: The Bill of Rights
http://constitutionalrights.constitutioncenter.org/app/home/writing

Index

About the Author

Matt Bowers is a writer and illustrator who lives in Minnesota. When he's not writing or drawing, he enjoys skiing, sailing, and going on adventures with his family. He hopes readers will continue to learn about government and be leaders in their communities.